D0854568

LIVES IN CRISIS

The African-American Slave Trade

R. G. GRANT

HODDER
Wayland

an imprint of Hodder Children's Books

Published in Great Britain in 2002 by
Hodder Wayland, an imprint of Hodder Children's Books.

This book was prepared for Hodder Wayland by Ruth Nason.

Series concept: Alex Woolf
Series design: Carole Binding

British Library Cataloguing in Publication Data
Grant, R. G.
   The African-American slave trade. - (Lives in crisis)
   1. Slave trade - Africa - History - Juvenile literature
   2. Slave trade - America - History - Juvenile literature
   I. Title
   382.4'4'09
ISBN 0 7502 4028 8

Printed in Hong Kong by Wing King Tong

Hodder Children's Books
A division of Hodder Headline Limited
338 Euston Road, London NW1 3BH

Acknowledgements

The Author and Publishers thank the following for their permission to reproduce photographs: Bridgeman Art Library: cover background and pages 3 and 30 (British Library, London, UK), and pages 10 (Museo Archeologico Nazionale, Naples, Italy), 12t (Bibliotheque Nationale, Paris, France), 12b (private collection), 20 (Royal Albert Memorial Museum, Exeter, Devon, UK), 24 (Wilberforce House, Hull City Museums and Art Galleries, UK); Camera Press: pages 4t, 26; Corbis Images: cover (right) and pages 1 and 59 (Macduff Everton), 4b (Bettmann), 6 (Bettmann), 7 (Bettmann), 8, 9t (Bettmann), 9b (Bettmann), 13 (Bettmann), 14 (Dave G. Houser), 16, 17, 18 (Bettmann), 21 (Bettmann), 23 (Bojan Brecelj), 25 (Bettmann), 27, 28, 29, 32, 33, 34 (Tony Arruza), 35 (Bettmann), 36t (E. O. Hoppé), 36b (Richard Cummins), 37 (Bettmann), 38t (Bettmann), 38b (Bettmann), 40-41 (Underwood & Underwood), 43 (Bettmann), 44 (Angelo Hornak), 45, 46t (Bettmann), 46b, 48b, 49, 50l (Bettmann), 50r (Bettmann), 51 (Bettmann), 53, 54 (Nathan Benn), 56t (Bettmann), 56b, 57 (James Davis; Eye Ubiquitous), 59t (Oscar White); Popperfoto/Reuters: pages 42, 55, 58.

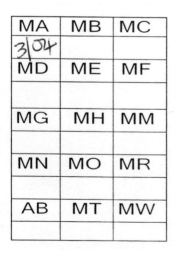

Cover (right) and page 1: part of a monument commemorating the abolition of slavery in Puerto Rico in 1873.

CONTENTS

Harvesting sugar cane in
Antigua, one of the sugar
islands of the West Indies.

SLAVERY AND FREEDOM, 1776

In 1999, descendants of Thomas Jefferson and of one of his slaves, Sally Hemings, gathered at the plantation Jefferson owned in Virginia. Jefferson (below), one of the founders of the USA, was almost certainly the father of several of Sally Hemings' children.

In 1776 the representatives of thirteen British colonies in North America declared their independence, founding the United States of America (USA). Their Declaration of Independence opened with a resounding pronouncement on freedom and human rights, penned by the idealistic Thomas Jefferson. It stated 'that all men are created equal and independent, that from that equal creation they derive rights inherent and inalienable, among which are the preservation of life and liberty, and the pursuit of happiness'.

Yet Jefferson owned black slaves – about 200 of them. The future first US president, George Washington, was also a slave-owner. Indeed, the majority of the leaders of the new USA, founded on the principle of freedom, either owned slaves or had taken part in the slave trade.

Freedom for all

In 1775 the English radical Tom Paine, one of the most outspoken supporters of the American Revolution, wrote a fierce denunciation of slavery. Expressing surprise that civilized Christians should approve of or be involved in this 'savage practice', he pointed out the contrast with Americans' desire for freedom from oppressive British rule:

'[I] entreat Americans to consider ... with what consistency or decency they complain so loudly of attempts to enslave *them*, while they hold so many hundred thousands in slavery, and annually enslave many thousands more ...'
(Paine, *African Slavery in America*)

The American leaders were in good company. Eighteenth-century Britain liked to call itself the 'home of liberty', but many of its aristocrats and its merchants had grown rich on the profits from goods produced by slave labour in the British-ruled islands of the West Indies. More than half of the approximately 70,000 Africans transported across the Atlantic against their will every year were carried in British ships. Other European countries were also heavily involved in slavery and the slave trade – primarily France and Portugal, but also Spain, the Netherlands, Denmark and Sweden.

In 1776 there were almost three million black slaves in the Americas, mostly concentrated in the European colonies of the West Indies and Brazil, and the southern USA. About one in five of the population of the new United States was a slave. In West Indian islands such as Barbados and Jamaica, slaves made up the majority of the population. Bought and sold like farm animals or furniture, slaves worked in labour gangs on large estates

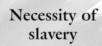

Necessity of slavery

Charles Pinckney, one of US President George Washington's closest associates, argued that slavery was a necessity in the USA:

'Negroes are to this country what raw materials are to another country ... No planter can cultivate his land without slaves.'

Keen to buy

Slaves in the Americas were traded like any commodity. In 1853 a Kentucky slave trader put the following advertisement in a newspaper:

'The undersigned wishes to purchase a large lot of NEGROES for the New Orleans market. I will pay $1200 to $1250 for No. 1 young men, and $850 to $1,000 for No. 1 young women. In fact I will pay more for likely [attractive] NEGROES than any other trader in Kentucky.' (Quoted in Coleman Jr, *Slavery Times in Kentucky*)

(known as 'plantations'), acted as butlers and man-servants, coachmen and cooks in large households, staffed riverboats and dockyards, and worked as artisans in towns and cities.

The work that slaves did, as well as the trade in slaves, was central to international economic life. In Europe and North America, people had developed a taste for small luxuries such as sugar, coffee and tobacco. Almost all these consumer goods

On a coffee plantation in Costa Rica, slaves spread husked coffee beans to dry in the sun.

were produced on plantations by the use of slave labour. An extremely profitable pattern of trade had developed. Goods from Europe or the northern USA were carried to the west coast of Africa and exchanged for slaves, who were shipped across the Atlantic for sale to plantation owners in Brazil, the West Indies and the southern USA. The products of the plantations were carried to the ports of Europe or the northern USA, where they commanded a premium price. In turn, goods from Europe and North America were sold to the plantation owners – equipment for their estates, food and clothing for the overseers and the slaves.

An immense number of white people in Europe and the New World were involved in slavery and the slave trade in some way. Most directly involved were the people who owned slaves or were employed to supervise them and those who commanded and manned the slave ships. But then there were the merchants who ran the trade and took the largest profits, the bankers and insurers who handled the financial side of the business, manufacturers who profited from shipping their products to Africa or the plantations, and monarchs and politicians who backed the trade and took their cut. Even consumers benefited from slavery each time they drank a cup of sweetened coffee.

In the eighteenth century the gentlemen who went to Lloyd's coffee house in the city of London benefited from slavery in two ways: they made money out of insuring ships that carried slaves, and they enjoyed coffee produced by slave labour.

The elegant cities of Bristol and Liverpool, Bordeaux and Nantes, Copenhagen and Boston, were full of new building that reflected the wealth the slave trade and slave-produced goods had brought.

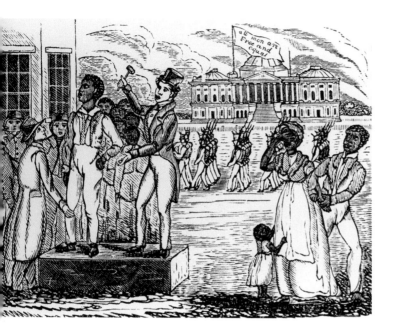

This engraving contrasts the ideals of the USA – expressed on the flag in the background – with the harsh reality of a slave auction.

Slavery challenged

At the time of the American Declaration of Independence, this state of affairs was just beginning to be seriously challenged. Many white people in Europe and North America regretted that they had ever become so dependent on the institution of slavery. The founders of the USA and other enlightened white gentlemen of the time were conscious that treating human beings as property, without rights, was hard to square with their Christian and humane principles. Just as importantly, they feared that the slaves, who were a majority in many places, might revolt and take revenge on their white masters. And they had begun to believe that slavery might not be as economically efficient as free labour.

Someone has to do it

An American slave trader, Richard Drake, recorded a conversation that he had with a ship's captain during a slaving voyage in the early nineteenth century:

'Leclerc and I had a chat about this African business [the slave trade]. He says he's repugnant to it, and I confess it's not a thing I like. But as my uncle argues, slaves must be bought and sold; somebody must do the trading; and why not make hay while the sun shines?' (Quoted in Pope-Hennessy, *Sins of the Fathers*)

But the leap to freeing all slaves seemed to them an awesomely difficult one to take, and was of course vehemently opposed by most of those who benefited financially from slavery.

In total, between 1500 and 1870, some 12 million captives were shipped from Africa, destined for sale in the New World. Over a million and a half died on the 'Middle Passage', as the voyage was called – about one in eight of those who embarked. African-American slavery surpassed any previous slave system in history, both in its size and in the intensity with which it exploited slave labour.

This book will explain how the Atlantic slave trade and slavery in the Americas grew to the proportions they did and how Europeans and white North Americans justified this to themselves. It will examine the impact of the slave trade on Africa, and the sufferings and resistance of the slaves themselves. Finally, it will describe the process by which the Atlantic slave trade and the institution of American slavery were abolished, and look at the long shadow that slavery has cast down to the present day.

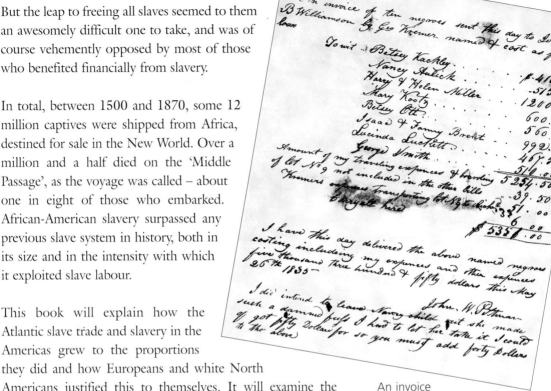

An invoice for the sale of ten slaves to an American plantation in 1835.

Three former slaves photographed in the late nineteenth century.

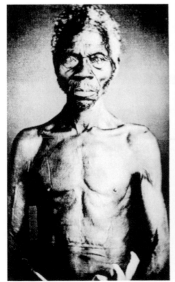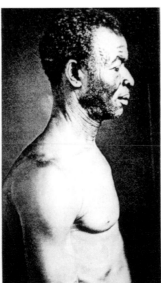

HOW THE ATLANTIC SLAVE TRADE GREW

A Roman slave girl carries in food for a banquet, in this painting from the first century at Herculaneum in southern Italy.

Some form of slavery existed in most human societies from the earliest days of civilization up to modern times. There was, historically, no special link between slavery and the colour of a person's skin. Europe was as much a source of slaves and a site of slavery as any other continent. One of the largest slave-owning societies in history was Ancient Rome. When the Roman Empire was at its height, around two thousand years ago, slaves made up about a third of the population of Italy, working as labourers in mines and on large rural estates, and staffing the households of wealthy city-dwellers. Slaves came from all the lands that the Romans conquered, including Britain and the rest of northwestern Europe.

After the fall of the Roman Empire, in the European Middle Ages, northwestern Europe became a virtually slave-free zone – an unusual situation. But slavery remained commonplace around the Mediterranean, where Christians fought Muslims in a long battle for domination. Christians enslaved Muslims and Muslims enslaved Christians – both sides believed that you should not make slaves of people of your own religion. The Venetians, in particular, used slaves on a considerable scale to work sugar estates on the Mediterranean islands of Cyprus and Crete. But the Muslim states around the Mediterranean provided by far the largest market for slaves. As well as tens of thousands of Christian slaves, they imported large numbers of black slaves from Africa south of the Sahara.

The green shading shows the Muslim states around the Mediterranean in about 1200, a major market for black slaves.

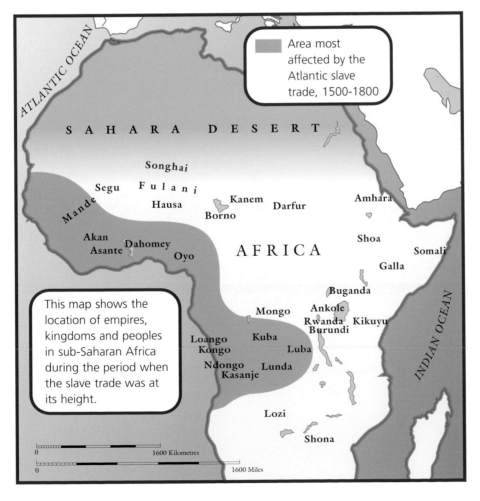

Area most affected by the Atlantic slave trade, 1500-1800

This map shows the location of empires, kingdoms and peoples in sub-Saharan Africa during the period when the slave trade was at its height.

Slaves in Africa

This illustration from a thirteenth-century Persian book shows Muslims buying and selling black slaves.

An African carving of slaves, on a chair seat made in the nineteenth century.

At the time of the European Middle Ages, sub-Saharan Africa was a place of varied cultures and societies, ranging from large and sophisticated empires to simpler groups of farmers or hunter-gatherers. As in most of the rest of the world, slavery existed there. African states fought one another in wars or raided their neighbours, carrying off captives who became slaves. In some African societies, people who had committed crimes were made into slaves as a punishment. And people might become slaves as a result of failure to pay their debts. Being a slave in Africa was not necessarily a tough lot in life. It did not necessarily mean that you did hard manual labour or were badly treated. But it did usually mean you could be bought and sold.

There was a flourishing trade in slaves between sub-Saharan African states, as well as a long-distance slave trade that took black Africans from the slave market at Timbuktu across the Sahara to north Africa. Other black slaves were carried to the Middle East from ports in east Africa. By the fifteenth century

up to 10,000 slaves a year were being transported along the Saharan caravan routes, mostly women and children, to serve in the courts of princes and other wealthy households in Muslim states around the Mediterranean. Along with them, in the camel caravans, went other precious goods such as gold and ivory.

Portuguese and Spanish traders

Christian Europeans were aware of the wealth of the Saharan trade and jealous of its control by the Muslim enemy. In the fifteenth century, the Christian rulers of Portugal sent sailors on voyages down the west coast of Africa. One of their main motives was to try to locate the source of the goods traded across the Sahara, especially gold. Although they had not set off in search of slaves, from the 1440s humans became part of Portuguese sailors' cargoes.

The Portuguese initially tried to capture Africans in raids on the coast, but it soon became clear that the local people were not prepared to be preyed upon. Apart from their ability as sailors, the Portuguese were not significantly superior to the Africans in technology or organization. They had no choice but to negotiate and trade with African rulers and merchants as equals. The peoples of west Africa were on the whole quite happy to trade with the Portuguese and the other Europeans who later followed them. The Africans' long-established patterns of local and long-distance trade could easily be adapted to selling to, and buying from, the new seaborne arrivals. Soon the Portuguese had built up a flourishing African commerce, primarily in gold and ivory, but also in slaves.

The caravel was a sailing vessel developed by the Portuguese in the fifteenth century, and used to explore the coast of Africa.

A statue of Christopher Columbus, in Puerto Rico.

The New World

Initially the market for African slaves was limited. Most were taken to Portugal and Spain, where they were primarily used as servants. When the Portuguese and Spanish took over Atlantic islands such as the Canaries, Cape Verde, Madeira and Sao Tome during the fifteenth century, these became a new destination for slaves. But it was only after Christopher Columbus sailed across the Atlantic in 1492, opening up the Americas to European conquest, that demand for slaves really began to take off.

The Spanish took the lead in occupying the New World. At first, they thought they would exploit their conquests by using the labour of the continent's native peoples. But these 'Indians' died in massive numbers, of diseases unwittingly brought to the New World by the Europeans. Those who survived often resisted being put to work, and also won the protection of Christian missionaries, who obstructed their enslavement and ruthless exploitation. At the same time, it proved impossible to find enough Spanish peasants or workers prepared to move to the New World. By the 1550s, thousands of slaves from Africa were being imported into the Spanish colonies of central and south America, where they performed a wide variety of jobs. Many lived in towns and cities as skilled artisans or household servants.

Letter from a king

One of the main sources of slaves in the early days of the Atlantic trade was the kingdom of the Kongo, in west central Africa. In 1540 the ruler of the Kongo, known to the Portuguese as King Afonso, wrote a letter to the king of Portugal pointing out how keen he was to encourage the slave trade:

'No king in all these parts esteems Portuguese goods as much as we do. We favour the trade, sustain it, open ... roads, and markets where the pieces [slaves] are traded.'
(Quoted in Thomas, *The Slave Trade*)

The Portuguese also had a colony in the Americas: Brazil. From the late sixteenth century, sugar production began to develop there, creating a need for large numbers of labourers to work on sugar plantations. As in the Spanish colonies, disease had decimated the native population and free labourers from Europe were not queuing up to emigrate across the Atlantic. African slaves provided an economically viable alternative source of labour. By the 1630s, there were almost 200,000 slaves in Brazil, producing the lion's share of the sugar consumed in Europe.

Up to this time, the Atlantic slave trade was still a relatively small-scale business. Muslim traders were still carrying as many African slaves across the Sahara as Europeans were shipping from the Atlantic coast. The major difference between the Atlantic trade and the older-established Saharan trade was that the Europeans preferred male slaves to women and children. Slaves were largely a by-product of wars between Africans that happened for quite other reasons. From time to time the supply of slaves on one part of the coast might dry up, during a period of peace and stability, and European slave-traders would have to shift to another area where wars were going on and therefore slaves were to be had. The overall impact of Europeans on Africa at this time was small. For example, the defeat of the Songhai Empire by an army from Morocco in 1591 was a far greater event in African terms than the establishment of European coastal trading posts.

European colonies in the Americas by about 1770.

- British
- French
- Dutch
- Portuguese
- Spanish

No trade

Acceptance of trading in human beings did not necessarily come naturally to Europeans. The British were to become the greatest slave-traders of all, but only after greed overcame their scruples. An English merchant, Richard Jobson, described how he had firmly turned down an offer of slaves from a west African chief in the 1620s:

'I made answer, we were a people who did not deal in any such commodities, nor did we buy or sell one another, or any that had our own shape.'
(Quoted in Blackburn, *The Making of New World Slavery*)

More slaves for the new colonies

This engraving was intended to explain how sugar was made in the French West Indies in 1667. Slaves not only planted and harvested sugar cane, but also worked at crushing and processing the cane to extract sugar.

From the second half of the seventeenth century the Atlantic slave trade grew to quite new proportions as Britain and France began to exploit their newly won colonies in the West Indies, such as Barbados and Jamaica for the British, and Martinique and Saint Domingue (now Haiti) for the French. Keen to imitate the success of the Portuguese in Brazil, the British and French established sugar plantations on the Caribbean islands, which were soon being worked by slave

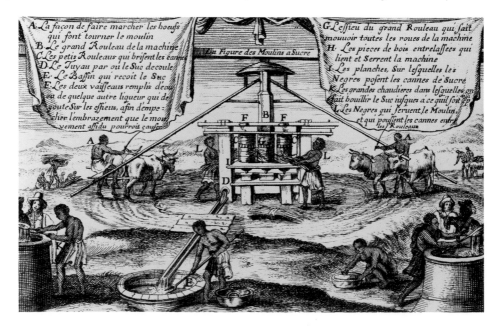

labourers imported from Africa. Europe's demand for sugar was insatiable, and so in turn was the sugar planters' demand for slaves.

Until this time, although sailors of other countries had made isolated slaving voyages (including Englishman Sir John Hawkyns in the 1560s), the Portuguese dominated the Atlantic slave trade that they had begun. But now first the Dutch, and then British, French and Danish traders moved in on the slave trade in force. The slave-trading nations established forts along the African coast, designed to defend themselves against their European rivals rather than against the local people. The African rulers and traders who provided the slaves grew increasingly wealthy because they were able to play off rival European customers against one another.

At first, Britain's colonies in North America – the future USA – looked as if they might follow a different pattern of development from Brazil and the West Indies. These colonies were able to attract a steady flow of immigrants from Europe, most brought in as 'indentured servants': in return for the cost of their passage across the Atlantic, they were pledged to work for a master for a fixed period of years before receiving their freedom. But from the late seventeenth century, as European immigrants increasingly demanded better treatment and

Sir John Hawkyns (1532-95) was the first Englishman to trade in slaves between west Africa and the West Indies.

Beneficial slavery

It was common for Europeans to justify the slave trade as a way of saving blacks from the supposed barbarism of their homeland. In 1592 a Spanish official in South America wrote of the slaves:

'It is very helpful to those wretches to save them from Guinea's [West Africa's] fire and tyranny and barbarism and brutality, where without law or god they live like savage beasts. Brought to a healthier land they should be very content, the more so as they will be kept and live in good order and religion from which they will derive many ... spiritual advantages.'
(Quoted in Blackburn, *The Making of New World Slavery*)

Ordained by God

Those involved in the slavery business were constantly looking for religious justification for their activities. John Pinney, a young English sugar planter who arrived in the West Indies in the 1760s, described how he came to accept slavery:

'I can assure you that I was shocked at the first appearance of human flesh exposed to sale. But surely God ordained them for the use and benefit of us. Otherwise his divine will would have made itself manifest by some particular sign or token.'
(Quoted in Thomas, *The Slave Trade*)

The arrival of twenty African slaves sold by a Dutch ship to the British colony at Jamestown, Virginia, in 1619.

conditions, African slaves were brought in to fill the need for a workforce on plantations producing tobacco in Virginia and Maryland and rice and indigo in the Carolinas. At the same time, enterprising merchants and sailors from New England colonies such as Massachusetts and Rhode Island started to carve out for themselves a profitable share in the Atlantic slave trade.

European governments actively promoted the slave trade, seeing it as essential to the development of their colonies. For example, in 1672 the British monarchy awarded the Royal African Company (RAC) the right to trade slaves to the British colonies. Many leading figures in British society had shares in the RAC, including the philosopher John Locke, whose writings are considered the foundation of most modern ideas on individual freedom. There were some doubts about the trade expressed by both religious and legal authorities in Europe. But mostly it was accepted as a normal part of the trade in goods and necessary to the development of colonies that would otherwise have been unexploited.

In the seventeenth century about two million slaves were carried across the Atlantic. The following century the number tripled to over six million. People had become by far the most valuable African export. From Senegal in the north to Angola in the south, African rulers and traders strove to satisfy the

No scruples

John Newton was an eighteenth-century English slave-ship captain who later quit the slave trade and became an abolitionist. He described how universally accepted slaving was in his early days:

'I think I should have quitted it sooner, had I considered it as I now do, to be unlawful and wrong. But I never had a scruple on this head at the time; nor was such a thought once suggested to me by a friend.'
(Quoted in Pope-Hennessy, *Sins of the Fathers*)

ever-expanding demand for slaves. Powerful African warrior states such as the kingdoms of Dahomey, Oyo and Asante rose on the back of the trade, as the military expansion of their empires produced a flow of captives to be sold along the coast. Their customers – the merchants and sea captains of ports such as Liverpool, Nantes, Lisbon, and Newport, Rhode Island – also prospered as the slave trade boomed. Meanwhile their victims, the millions of forced migrants to the New World, suffered and struggled helplessly against their fate.

Elegant traders in slaves

The French port of Nantes played a leading part in the slave trade. An observer described the pride and elegance of the city's wealthy slave-traders in the eighteenth century:

'They form a class apart, never mixing, save when business requires it, with the other merchants, who approach them with signs of a profound respect ... They are important personages, leaning on high, gilt-topped canes ... their hair carefully arranged and powdered, with suits made of dark- or light-coloured silks ... wearing long waistcoats and breeches, also of silk, and white stockings and shoes with large gold or silver buckles ...'
(Quoted in Thomas, *The Slave Trade*)

HOW THE SLAVE TRADE WORKED

Capturing slaves

Throughout the time of the Atlantic slave trade, most Africans became slaves in ways that were familiar in African societies – chiefly through warfare, or as a punishment for some crime or misdemeanour, or as a consequence of falling into debt. But the existence of a vast demand for slaves gave a fresh incentive for powerful African states to wage war, or to carry out raids on neighbouring peoples with the sole aim of carrying captives off into slavery. Where slave-raiding was most intense – for example, on the borders of the Asante and Dahomey kingdoms – whole regions were depopulated. In much of west and central Africa, life for peaceful villagers became increasingly insecure, as groups of bandits roved the countryside looking for people to kidnap for sale to slave-traders.

Former slave Olaudah Equiano became a leader of the anti-slavery movement in Britain at the end of the eighteenth century.

Kidnapped

Born in the Gambia, West Africa, in the eighteenth century, Olaudah Equiano was enslaved and carried across the Atlantic. He later gained his freedom and wrote a vivid account of his life. It includes a description of how, as children in their village, he and his sister were kidnapped to be sold as slaves:

'One day, when all our people were gone to their works as usual, and only I and my dear sister were left to mind the house, two men and a woman got over our walls and, in a moment, seized us both and, without giving us time to cry out, they stopped our mouths, and ran off with us into the nearest wood. Here they tied our hands and continued to carry us as far as they could.'
(Equiano et al., *Slave Narratives*)

No sellers without buyers

Although most Africans' first experience of slavery was at the hands of other Africans, this does not lessen the responsibility that Europeans or North Americans bear for the slave trade. As freed slave Ottobah Cugoana wrote in 1780:

'I must own, to the shame of my own countrymen, that I was first kidnapped and betrayed by my own complexion [i.e. by other blacks], who were the first cause of my exile and slavery; but if there were no buyers there would be no sellers.'
(Quoted in Pope-Hennessy, *Sins of the Fathers*)

Most slaves came from inland, brought long distances on foot to the slave-trading ports. Some were used as porters, being forced to carry other trade goods such as ivory to the coast. The journey generally followed well-established trade routes and might be broken by long stops at villages along the way. Slaves were sometimes bought and sold several times in the course of the journey, so the trader who finally sold them to the Europeans had no contact with the person who had originally owned or enslaved them. An unknown number of slaves must have died during these forced marches, of disease or ill-treatment. Arriving at the coast, the survivors were held in barracoons – a form of temporary prison – awaiting sale.

African slaves on their way to the coast.

'A very unwholesome place'

Large numbers of European seamen and slave-traders died along the African coast, mostly of tropical diseases. In a letter sent to England from the Gambia, one slave-ship captain wrote:

'Since our coming into this river it hath pleased the Lord to afflict us with much sickness that we have buried three and twenty men. My chief and my second mates and bosun are three of them ... It is a very unwholesome place that we are burnt up for want of air and breezes ... I never see men die so suddenly in my life.'
(Quoted in Craton, *Sinews of Empire*)

Used as money through much of Africa, cowrie shells were among the items brought to the African coast by traders to exchange for slaves.

On the whole, Europeans played no direct part in capturing slaves or bringing them to the coast. There were important exceptions – in the region of the Congo and Angola, in particular, the Portuguese penetrated far inland, organizing both the purchase of slaves and slave raids. But mostly Europeans stayed close to their ships on the coast. They might on occasion loan goods to an African trader, who would travel inland to buy slaves on their behalf. Generally, though, they just waited for slaves to be brought to the coast for sale.

Buying and selling

For the Europeans or North Americans, involvement in the slave trade normally began as a business decision to embark on a high-risk venture. Sending a slave ship to Africa was an enterprise requiring the investment of a good deal of capital that could be, and frequently was, lost. Typically, a group of businessmen got together to employ a captain and a crew of 20 or 30 and fit out a ship. The most expensive part of the business was buying trade goods. African merchants were very particular as to the goods they were prepared to accept. A typical cargo for trading on the African coast might include textiles, often top-quality goods imported from Asia; cowrie shells, also brought from the East by the Europeans and used in much of Africa as a form of money; guns; various alcoholic

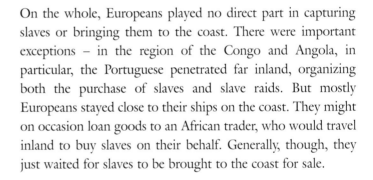

Skilful traders

Writing in 1682, a French slave-trader, Jean Barbot, described how it had become impossible to fool Africans into accepting shoddy goods in exchange for slaves:

'The blacks of the Gold Coast are very skilled in the nature and the proper qualities of all the Europeans' wares and merchandise vended [sold] there ... they examine everything with as much prudence and ability as any European trader can do.'
(Quoted in Pope-Hennessy, *Sins of the Fathers*)

drinks – Africans were partial to rum from Rhode Island and French brandy; and bar iron that African blacksmiths used to make tools and weapons.

When the ship arrived at the African coast, the business of buying and selling began. It was usually an extremely lengthy process. Slaves were typically bought in small lots of five or six at a time. It could take over six months for a ship to exchange its wares for a full cargo of 300 to 600 slaves. During that time the ship might shift up and down the coast in search of local traders who had slaves for sale.

European and North American slave-traders by no means had the upper hand in their dealings with Africans. They often paid heavy taxes to African rulers both for the right to trade and for each slave exported. Local African traders drove a hard bargain, like shrewd business people everywhere. Most Europeans and

Tippu Tib was a slave trader in Zanzibar from the mid-nineteenth century to the early twentieth. At one time he owned as many as 10,000 slaves.

North Americans thought African customs 'barbarous' and many expressed a racial contempt for African people. But traders who made frequent visits to Africa or who lived there for long periods as 'factors' at trading posts often struck up friendly relationships with local people. They were invited as guests to feasts or ceremonies and received customary African hospitality. In return, some African traders and princes travelled as guests to merchants' homes in Europe or North America, or sent their children for education there.

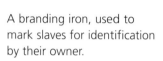

Most traders, both black and white, seem to have found it easy to ignore the abject fear and despair of the slaves whom they bought and sold. Already torn from their homes and kin, the slaves were subjected to a humiliating physical examination by traders keen for good-quality merchandise – that is, slaves free of disease and capable of years of hard labour. Once bought, the slaves were usually branded like cattle, so that the purchaser could be sure that the captives delivered to his ship were the same ones he had paid for.

A branding iron, used to mark slaves for identification by their owner.

Setting sail

When a full cargo of slaves had been got together, the ship was ready to set sail. The captain and crew regarded this as a

Leaving Africa

Olaudah Equiano gave the following account of his first hours on board a slave ship about to set off across the Atlantic:

'Amongst the poor chained men I found some of my own nation, which in a small degree gave ease to my mind. I inquired of these what was to be done with us? They gave me to understand we were to be carried to these white people's country to work for them ... But still I feared I should be put to death, the white people looked and acted, as I thought, in so savage a manner; for I had never seen among any people such instances of brutal cruelty; and this shewn not only to us blacks, but also to some of the whites themselves ... At last, when the ship we were in had got all of her cargo, they made ready with many fearful noises, and we were all put under deck ...'
(Equiano et al., *Slave Narratives*)

Slave mutiny

Writing in 1734, a British slave-ship captain described how the captain of another ship had been killed by the slaves he was transporting:

'Being in the forecastle of the ship, amongst the men negroes when they were eating their vitals [food], they laid hold on him, and beat out his brains with the little tubs, out of which they eat their boiled rice. This mutiny having been plotted amongst all the grown negroes on board, they ran to the fore part of the ship in a body ... So that at last the chief mate was obliged to order one of the quarter-deck guns ... to be fired amongst them; which occasioned a terrible destruction. For there were nearly 80 negroes killed and drowned, many jumping overboard when the gun was fired.'
(Quoted in Craton, *Sinews of Empire*)

particularly dangerous moment in their enterprise. They were terrified of an uprising by the slaves on board, who greatly outnumbered them. Such mutinies most commonly happened while the ship was still close to the African shore, when slaves were gripped by terror at embarking into the unknown, and inspired by a last hope of escaping to land.

This image of slaves packed on board a ship was used by the British anti-slavery movement as propaganda in its campaign to abolish the slave trade in the late eighteenth century.

In 1839, there was a slave revolt on a ship called the *Amistad*. This is a still from a Steven Spielberg film, *Amistad*, made in 1998.

With crews watchful and most slaves kept manacled together below deck, few mutinies succeeded. And when they failed, vicious punishments were inflicted on attempted 'mutineers', usually in front of the rest of the slaves, so they would know what to expect if they attempted the same.

Limits of inhumanity

Writing a journal of a voyage by the slave ship *Hannibal* in 1694, Captain Thomas Phillips revealed not only how unspeakably brutal slavers could be, but also that some were definitely more humane than others:

'I have been informed that some commanders have cut off the legs or arms of the most wilful [slaves], to terrify the rest ... I was advised by some of my officers to do the same, but I could not be persuaded ... to put in practice such barbarity and cruelty to poor creatures who ... are as much the works of God's hands, and no doubt as dear to him as ourselves.'
(Quoted in Thomas, *The Slave Trade*)

The fear of a slave mutiny was probably the main cause of mistreatment of slaves on the voyage. Even a relatively humane slave-ship captain reported that he treated his human cargo only 'with as much humanity as a regard to my own safety would admit'.

The Middle Passage

The horrors of the 'Middle Passage' across the Atlantic are well documented. Many of the slaves were in a state of total despair. There are many recorded instances of slaves jumping overboard to die by drowning. Some tried to commit suicide by hunger strike, and the crews kept a careful watch to see that slaves ate their rations. Refusal to eat would result in a vicious beating. The overall hopelessness of the slaves' fate was compounded by a host of smaller evils, from the casual brutality of the crew to constant sea-sickness. The degree of overcrowding in the slave quarters varied from

The overcrowding and lack of air and light below decks on a slave ship made disease more likely to spread.

Scenes of horror

Writing in 1788, Alexander Falconbridge, a British surgeon, described the nightmare conditions during a slave voyage on which he was ship's doctor:

'Some wet and blowing weather having occasioned the port-holes to be shut ... fluxes [dysentery] and fevers among the negroes ensued ... My profession requiring it, I frequently went down among them, till at length their apartments became so extremely hot as to be only sufferable for a very short time ... The deck, that is the floor of their rooms, was so covered with the blood and mucous which had proceeded from them in consequence of the flux, that it resembled a slaughterhouse. It is not in the power of the human imagination to picture to itself a situation more dreadful or disgusting.' (Quoted in Pope-Hennessy, *Sins of the Fathers*)

ship to ship, but was always sufficient to create stifling heat during bad weather when all openings had to be closed. Few ships managed to carry truly sufficient quantities of food and water for perhaps 500 people on a voyage of two months and upward to the West Indies.

Thrown overboard – probably because of an infectious disease.

Of course, slave-ship captains had a financial interest in seeing as many slaves as possible arrive in the New World alive and well. On a well-run ship, once out on the ocean the slaves were usually allowed on deck during daylight hours, under strict surveillance, and their quarters were regularly cleaned. But, at least until the end of the eighteenth century, even a humane and careful captain had no answer to the main killer on the Middle Passage, which was disease – chiefly dysentery (known as 'the flux') and smallpox. Ship's doctors were employed to keep the valuable human cargo alive, but they understood little of the causes of disease and had no viable cures to offer. At the first sign of contagious disease the slaves affected would be thrown overboard and left to drown. About one in eight slaves on average died on an Atlantic crossing, although this figure masks wide variations from voyage to voyage.

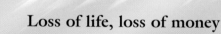

Loss of life, loss of money

In his 1694 journal of the voyage of the slave ship *Hannibal*, Captain Thomas Phillips lamented the financial loss that resulted as smallpox and dysentery ravaged crew and slaves alike:

'We spent in our passage ... two months eleven days ... in which time there happened much sickness and mortality among my poor men [crew] and negroes, that of the first we buried 14, and of the last 320 ... whereby the loss in all amounted to near 6,560 pounds sterling.'
(Quoted in Pope-Hennessy, *Sins of the Fathers*)

Slaves for sale

An English doctor observed the sorry sight of slaves awaiting sale on arrival in a West Indian port:

'A newly imported cargo of 220 human beings was ... exposed for sale. They were crouched down upon their forms [benches] around a large room; during a visit of more than an hour that we were there not a word was uttered by one of them. On entering the room the eyes of all were turned towards us, as if to read in our countenances [faces] their fate; they were all nearly naked; ... with few exceptions they were but skin and bone.'
(Quoted in Ransford, *The Slave Trade*)

Slaves often formed strong bonds with those who shared their sufferings on the same voyage. This happened despite the fact that they came from many different African nations and different classes of African society – the sons of princes mixed with peasants. Slaves who had been shipmates for the long weeks of the crossing frequently managed to keep in touch and maintain friendships even after sale in the Americas. Their shipmates became like a new family to them.

Arrival off the coast of their destination in the New World brought slaves to a new pitch of anxiety, since they had no idea what awaited them. There was frequently a long wait as ships were put into quarantine to avoid importing disease. Selling the slaves was also sometimes a slow, long-drawn-out process, when buyers were in short supply or the slaves were considered of poor quality. But in the end slaves did not remain unsold. Even those who were sick would be taken off by speculators who bought them for next to nothing, on the off chance that they might recover. Once bought, slaves were likely to be branded for a second time, with the sign of their new owner. Then they were led off into a new life.

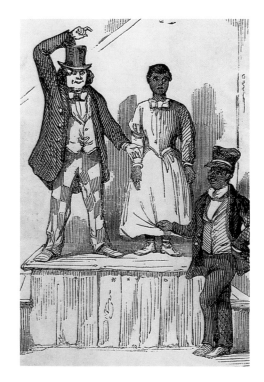

Selling a slave at auction, in Richmond, Virginia – an illustration from 1856.

SLAVERY IN THE NEW WORLD

With no control over their destinies, African slaves arriving in the Americas were subject to the lottery of fate. They might be sold to a 'good master' or a cruel tyrant. They might become a worker on a small farm or one of more than one hundred slaves on a large estate or plantation. They might find themselves in disease-ridden Surinam or in the relatively healthy climate of Virginia. But all Africans underwent a struggle to cope with their new situation. Probably about one in ten slaves died within 18 months of arrival in the Americas, a period callously known to slave owners as the 'seasoning'.

Caribbean sugar islands

The worst fate was to be sent to a sugar-cane plantation, as on Barbados and other Caribbean 'sugar islands'. Although Africans were used to the idea of slavery, nothing in their homeland had prepared them for the sort of conditions that prevailed on these plantations – a life of unremitting hard

Harvesting sugar cane, as here in Antigua in 1823, was a job that involved men, women and children.

Africa preferred

Ottobah Cugoana, a freed slave who wrote his memoirs in London in the 1780s, contrasted conditions in Africa with those on the slave plantations of the West Indies:

'So far as I can remember, some of the Africans in my country kept slaves, which they take in war or for debt; but those which they keep are well, and good care taken of them, and treated well ... I may safely say that all the poverty and misery that any of the inhabitants of Africa meet with among themselves is far inferior to [that] which they meet with in the West Indies, where their hard-hearted overseers have neither regard to the laws of God, nor the life of their fellow-men.'
(Quoted in Pope-Hennessy, *Sins of the Fathers*)

labour driven by fear of punishment. From the youngest children upwards, the slaves were not only subjected to back-breaking work all day long in gangs in the fields, but also had to carry out shift work through the night in the small sugar mills attached to each estate, where cane was processed.

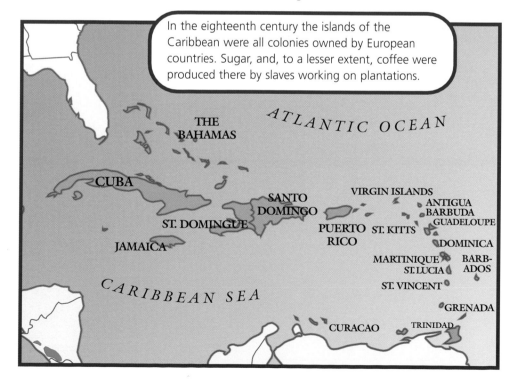

In the eighteenth century the islands of the Caribbean were all colonies owned by European countries. Sugar, and, to a lesser extent, coffee were produced there by slaves working on plantations.

During the five-month period of the annual sugar harvest, some slaves ended up working an 18-hour day. The sugar plantations often supplied little or no food to the slaves. They were expected to grow their own food on tiny plots of land allotted to them.

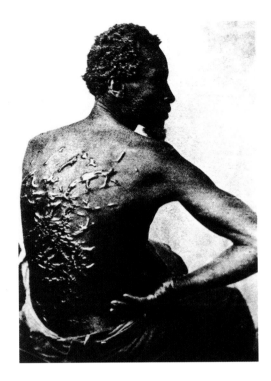

An early photograph shows the scars left by the lashes of a whip on a former slave's back.

West Indian sugar plantations were major enterprises in which landowners – often rich absentees living in Britain or France – had invested considerable capital and from which they expected substantial profits. The desire to maximize productivity for maximum profit was the main cause of cruelty. Overseers and slave-drivers had the job of extracting the maximum of effort from each slave, and in the absence of any other incentive to work hard, the slaves could be driven to it only by the threat of the lash. The slaves had no defence against any form of mistreatment or, in the case of women slaves, sexual exploitation.

The sugar plantations were constantly restocked with fresh slaves brought from Africa. This was partly because male slaves greatly outnumbered

On a sugar plantation

Janet Schaw, a genteel English lady, visited the Caribbean island of Antigua in the 1770s. She noted how work on the sugar plantations was arranged:

'The negroes who are all in troops are sorted so as to match each other in size and strength. Every ten negroes have a driver, who walks behind them, holding in his hand a short whip and a long one. You will easily guess the use of these weapons; a circumstance of all others the most horrid. They are naked, male and female down to the girdle [waist], and you constantly observe where application [of the whip] has been made.'
(Quoted in Blackburn, *The Making of New World Slavery*)

Merited punishments

Sir Hans Sloane, a distinguished English doctor and botanist, approved of the punishment of slaves that he had witnessed in Jamaica in the 1680s. Writing 20 years later, he described how slaves who rebelled would be burned or mutilated, and even those guilty only of not working well enough were brutally treated:

'For negligence they are usually whipped by the overseers with hard-wood switches, till they be all bloody. After they are whipped till they are raw, some put on their skins pepper and salt to make them smart ... These punishments are sometimes merited by the slaves, who are a very perverse generation of people, and though they appear harsh, yet are scarce equal to their crimes ...'
(Quoted in Blackburn, *The Making of New World Slavery*)

In about 1863, Wilson Chinn, a freed slave, posed for this photograph to show some of the equipment used to punish slaves.

female. A shortage of child-bearing women led to a very low birth rate. In any case, slave women on the plantations had few children. There was also a high death rate. Some plantation owners seem to have felt that it made better commercial sense to replenish slaves by purchase than to help them survive by feeding them adequately or giving them enough rest.

Uprisings

On the sugar islands slave masters and overseers were often heavily outnumbered. Given the way they treated their slaves, they not surprisingly lived in constant fear of an uprising. The majority of the slaves were young men, and many of them came from cultures in which the traditional role of a young man was to use weapons as a warrior and hunter. But it was hard for the slaves to organize a revolt. Not only were they unarmed and under constant surveillance, but they came from different African nations and initially had no common language. The planters of Barbados in the seventeenth century recognized that they had 'no greater security than the diversity of our negroes' languages'.

Descendants of maroons still form a strong community in Jamaica. Here they celebrate a 'Festival of the Maroons' in St Elizabeth Parish, 1992.

Despite all difficulties, there were major uprisings, for example in Antigua in 1736 and in Jamaica in 1760-1. But the well-organized and heavily armed forces at the disposal of the whites ensured the slaves' defeat. Defeated rebels were always subject to the most barbaric punishments by the colonial authorities – after the Antigua uprising, 77 slaves were burned alive and others were tied to gibbets and left to starve to death.

Fleeing into the forests and hills was a more feasible option than rebellion, and many slaves did slip away, becoming 'maroons'. On a large island such as Jamaica, groups of maroons survived permanently in remote areas, often waging low-level guerrilla warfare on the colonial authorities. But escape was always fraught with difficulty. An escapee would have to survive in harsh unfamiliar country, a prey to wild animals and insects, having to forage for food and drinkable water. As well as this daunting prospect, there was always the threat of vicious punishment if caught, which undoubtedly deterred many would-be escapers, as it was meant to do. In the end, slave resistance to white power most commonly took the form of a sullen go-slow at work. This required great courage, risking the overseer's lash, but sometimes it successfully won concessions in return for an agreement to raise the work tempo again.

Brazil and North America

Outside the West Indies, the largest concentrations of slaves were in Brazil and North America. In Brazil conditions of work for slaves could be just as frightful as in the Caribbean. As well as labouring on sugar plantations, slaves were used to sift gold from the streams of the Minas Gerais region. This was terrible work, involving standing in freezing cold water for many hours a day. As in the Caribbean, during the eighteenth century more slaves in Brazil died than were born.

Only in North America did the slave population expand through natural increase. One reason for this may be that sugar was not a major crop. The tobacco plantations of Virginia did not require such intensive labour for so much of the year. There was also less disease and better food available in North America – not only Africans but also white people had a higher life expectancy there than in the Caribbean or Brazil. But there

An anti-slavery engraving, produced in 1824, contrasts the life of a slave, forced to do hard labour, with the idleness of the plantation owner and his family.

Former slave quarters in Savannah, Georgia, photographed in 1926.

is no evidence that slaves in North America were fundamentally better treated than anywhere else in the New World. The whip was used as a form of discipline on many plantations, and other forms of mistreatment, such as the sexual abuse of slave women by whites, were common.

A new life

A reconstruction of slave quarters in Louisiana.

Despite the powerlessness of their condition, slaves did manage to make a life for themselves in the New World. On the plantations a newcomer took a place in a society which had its own hierarchy, with more experienced slaves entrusted with more responsible jobs and earning special privileges in return. One job that carried high status in the Caribbean slave world was that of muleteer, entrusted with carrying goods around the island on muleback, far from the plantation. Promotion to this sort of work was something to which a slave might aspire. Many slaves developed craft skills, becoming

From apprenticeship to auction

Being a slave could involve many different kinds of work and many different kinds of experience; the only common feature was a lack of control over your own destiny. William Craft, an escaped slave who published an account of his life in the USA in 1860, gives a vivid impression of the twists and turns of a slave's fate:

'My old master ... apprenticed a brother and myself out to learn trades: he to a blacksmith and myself to a cabinet-maker. If a slave has a good trade, he will let or sell for more than a person without one, and many slaveholders have their slaves taught trades on this account. But [then] my old master wanted money; so he mortgaged my sister and myself, then about 16, to one of the banks ... Time rolled on, the money became due, my master was unable to meet his payments; so the banks had us placed upon the auction stand and sold to the highest bidder.'
(Equiano et al., *Slave Narratives*)

blacksmiths or carpenters, for example. This might eventually allow them to earn some money of their own and win them a measure of independence. Slaves could also sometimes make money by selling the products of their vegetable plots in local Sunday markets.

The 'good master'

Some slave-owners saw themselves as humane and decent people, and made a conscious effort to treat their slaves well. Being owned by a 'good master' could make a big difference to a slave's life, even if it could not make up for the lack of freedom.

Phillis Wheatley, a slave in Boston, Massachusetts, had a talent for poetry. She was brought to England in 1773 and became the first black woman to have her work published in Britain.

Slaves who worked in households as cooks, maids and personal servants were generally much better treated than field workers on the plantations. So were slaves employed in towns and cities – for example, as dock-workers in the ports. Former slave Frederick Douglass wrote that 'a city slave ... is much better fed and clothed, and enjoys privileges altogether unknown to the slave on the plantation'. But however well treated they might be, all slaves knew they could be sold at any time – and sale always threatened them with separation from family and friends and an abrupt end to decent treatment.

The auction house in Atlanta, Georgia, photographed in about 1865.

Still just a slave

In his account of his life published in 1845, former slave Frederick Douglass described the fate of his grandmother, a household slave. Despite loyal and intimate service to a kind master from the cradle to the grave, she remained at his death just a piece of property to be passed on to his heirs:

'She had served my old master faithfully from youth to old age ... She had rocked him in infancy, attended him in childhood, served him though life, and at his death wiped from his icy brow the cold death-sweat, and closed his eyes forever. She was nevertheless a slave – a slave for life – a slave in the hands of strangers ...'
(Douglass, *Narrative of the Life of Frederick Douglass*)

Free 'people of colour'

At best, a slave might even gain his or her freedom. Over time a population of free 'people of colour' developed throughout the Americas. There were many routes to freedom – it could be bought, or earned as a reward for special service, or simply granted by a master on whim. Many black slave women had children fathered by their masters or other whites, and these mixed-race children were sometimes freed at birth. The chances of freedom depended on where a slave was. In Brazil by 1800 there was a large and growing free black and mulatto population. In the British West Indies, by the early nineteenth century, about one in ten of the coloured population was free. In North America, by contrast, there were relatively few free blacks.

Ironically, some free blacks themselves owned slaves – as did some Native Americans. And most whites were not slave-owners. Yet the identification between skin colour and personal status was very strong, especially in North America, where free 'people of colour' were always at risk of being seized by whites and taken back into slavery. As far as most people were concerned, being black simply meant being a slave.

A race below

Free 'people of colour' had to confront the barrier of racial discrimination. Writing in 1843, former slave Moses Granby described the reception he encountered in the non-slaveholding North of the USA:

'Although I was free as to the law, I was made to feel severely the difference between persons of different colours. No black man was admitted to the same seats in churches with the whites, nor to the inside of public conveyances, nor into street coaches or cabs ... We were treated as though we were of a race of men below the whites.'
(Granby, *Life of a Slave*)

Racism

Everywhere in the Americas racism developed as an excuse and a support for the slave system. Whites justified their exploitation of blacks as slaves by arguing that they were more animal than human and thus suitable to be treated like horses or pigs. Racism became even more important as the slave population, despite the opposition of most slave-owners, was gradually converted to Christianity. To justify ill-treatment and denial of rights to fellow Christians, whites had to argue that blacks were inferior by nature and

Barbarous natures

The white rulers of the American colonies justified the oppression of slaves by claiming that the Africans were by nature prone to violence and disorder. The preamble to the South Carolina slave legal code of 1696 stated:

'Whereas the plantation and estates of this Province cannot be well and sufficiently managed and brought into use, without the labour and service of negroes and other slaves; and forasmuch as the said negroes and other slaves ... are of barbarous, wild, savage natures ... constitutions, laws, and orders should in this Province be made and enacted ... as may restrain the disorders ... and inhumanity to which they are naturally prone and inclined.'
(Quoted in Stinchcombe, *Sugar Island Slavery in the Age of Enlightenment*)

would revert to 'barbarism' if not kept under strict discipline. Slavery was unconvincingly presented as a 'civilizing' influence. Upholding racism was especially important to poorer whites, whose only claim to be superior to freed slaves lay in the colour of their skin.

Uniting as one race

When slaves arrived in the New World, they saw themselves not as 'Africans' or 'blacks', but as, for example, Hausa or Akan or Ewe – different nations with different languages and customs. But through the shared experience of slavery and the pressure of white racism, they came to develop a common identity, creating a new culture out of a blend between African and European traditions. Having no shared African language, the slaves inevitably turned to the language of their masters as a common means of communication. But they mingled it with elements from African languages, so that in the Caribbean, for example, the 'Creole' versions of French or English that they spoke were often barely comprehensible to the whites.

Similarly, although slaves were converted to Christianity, African religions persisted under the surface. In Brazil and parts of the Caribbean, the practices of voodoo or candomble witchcraft came to coexist comfortably with the worship of

Catholic saints. The traditions of music and dance that the Africans carried with them across the Atlantic especially struck Europeans, who had never heard anything like their rhythmic drumming and chants. This too was to blend with European influences, to create blues, jazz and pop music in modern times.

The culture created by the forced immigrants from Africa was different in different parts of the Americas. Because in North America, at an early stage, a far higher proportion of the slaves were American-born, rather than fresh from Africa, the culture that developed there was significantly less 'African' than in the Caribbean or Brazil. But everywhere in the New World, the culture that the slaves created eventually made them into a new people, no longer fully African although still with African roots.

An everlasting system

The nature of slavery changed over time. By 1800, in all parts of the Americas, an increasing number of slaves were American-born. They had not been torn from another life in Africa, nor had they experienced the trauma of enslavement and transportation across the Atlantic. Some had never even been bought and sold – they remained the property of the master who had owned their mother and stayed where they had been born and raised. Especially in Brazil and the USA, where most plantation owners lived on their estates, the masters had known some of their slaves all their lives. No wonder many people, both slave-owners and slaves, felt that the slave system was destined to last for ever.

Punished for teaching

Most slaves were illiterate. Plantation owners tried to stop slaves learning to read and write, because education would make them harder to control. In Savannah, Georgia, a local ordnance stated:

'Any person that teaches a person of colour, slave or free, to read or write ... is subject to a fine of $30 for each offence; and every person of colour who keeps a school to teach reading and writing is subject to a fine of $30, or to be imprisoned for 10 days and whipped 39 lashes.'
(Quoted in Ransford, *The Slave Trade*)

Both before and after the aboltion of slavery, music was a favourite form of expression for African Americans of all ages.

THE STRUGGLE FOR ABOLITION

Slavery was a commercial success. The Atlantic slave trade made money for the people who ran it, and African slaves in the Americas performed the tasks required of them in an economical way. But in the late eighteenth century the slave system came under attack both from reformers in Europe and North America and from slaves and ex-slaves in revolt against their oppressors. Those who benefited from slavery were put on the defensive as the struggle for abolition gathered strength.

The winds of change

The shift of opinion in Europe and North America against slavery and the slave trade had varied roots. One factor was a change of attitude among committed Christians. Although Christian churches had traditionally supported slavery, by the 1780s Quakers, Methodists, Anglican evangelists and others

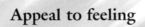

Appeal to feeling

Anti-slavery campaigners contrasted the sufferings of the Africans with the heartlessness of the slave-traders. In his *Thoughts Upon Slavery*, published in 1774, the Methodist leader John Wesley addressed himself to slave-ship captains, asking them:

'Do you never feel another's pain? Have you no sympathy? ... No pity for the miserable? When you saw the flowing eyes, the heaving breasts, or the bleeding sides or tortured limbs of your fellow beings, were you a stone or a brute ...?'
(Quoted in Thomas, *The Slave Trade*)

John Wesley.

Chosen by God

White anti-slavery campaigners were often insufferably self-righteous and adopted a piously superior attitude towards black slaves. One prominent British abolitionist, Sir Thomas Fowell Buxton, wrote in his diary:

'It has pleased God to place some duties upon me with regard to the poor slaves, and those duties I must not abandon. Oppression, cruelty, and persecution, and, what is worse, absence of religion, must not continue to grind that race through my neglect.'
(Quoted in Blackburn, *The Overthrow of Colonial Slavery*)

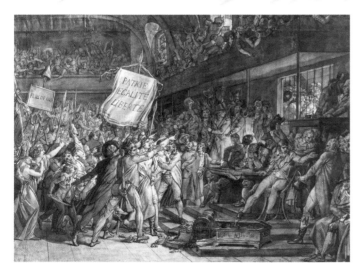

French revolutionaries calling for the death of King Louis XVI carry a banner with the words 'Country, Equality, Liberty' on it. In line with their principles, they declared an end to slavery in France's colonies.

were declaring slavery to be counter to Christian principles and campaigning vigorously against it. Slavery also ran counter to the ideas of individual freedom, equality and universal human rights which developed through the eighteenth century and came to the fore in the American and French revolutions. Even more important, the arguments of economists such as Adam Smith, who published his famous *Wealth of Nations* in 1776, were used to urge that free labour – that is, workers employed in return for wages – would be more economically beneficial than slavery. Last, but far from least, fear of slave rebellions convinced many whites that their safety required an end to a system that involved the oppression of millions by brute force.

Arguing for abolition

The first successes of the abolitionist movement came in banning slavery in places where it existed on a small scale and was of no economic importance. For example, the arguments of Quakers such as Anthony Benezet brought Pennsylvania to commit to abolishing slavery in 1780, and most other Northern states of the USA had followed suit by the end of the century.

William Wilberforce (1759-1833) led the anti-slavery movement in Britain from 1788. His memorial statue is in Westminster Abbey, London.

In Britain, in 1772, abolitionist Granville Sharp took up the case of James Somerset, a slave brought to England from Jamaica by his owner. Somerset escaped but was recaptured and destined to be sent back to the West Indies for sale. However, Lord Chief Justice Mansfield ruled that this could not be done. Although the ruling was far from clear-cut, it was widely taken as deciding that slavery was illegal on British soil.

From the 1780s, the anti-slavery movement in Britain concentrated on achieving the abolition of the slave trade, rather than of slavery. Leaders of the movement included Thomas Clarkson, former slave Olaudah Equiano, and William Wilberforce, an MP who carried the struggle into the House of Commons. In 1787, anti-slavery clubs were established throughout the country. The campaign became perhaps the first example of a modern-style mass political protest. Nonetheless, it proved a long and hard struggle. A large group of MPs, representing the interests of West Indian planters or merchants engaged in the slave trade, stubbornly resisted abolition. The British parliament did not finally agree to the banning of the slave trade until 1807.

Given Britain's leading role in the trade, this was a decisive moment. Denmark had already banned the slave trade in 1804, and the USA followed Britain's example in 1808. After the end of the Napoleonic Wars in 1815, Britain tried to extend the ban to all other countries and set up anti-

ABOLITION OF THE SLAVE TRADE, OR THE MAN THE MASTER.

A pro-slavery British cartoon of 1789 paints a grim picture of what would happen if the slave trade were abolished.

slavery patrols to intercept foreign slave ships. Despite this high-handed action, the trade still continued. Cuba was an especially fruitful customer for the slave-traders in the first half of the nineteenth century, taking more than 10,000 slaves a year. Brazil also continued to import slaves on a large scale, by this time primarily to work on coffee plantations. Many were shipped from ports in east Africa, mostly in present-day Mozambique. The Atlantic slave trade did not finally die out until the end of the 1860s, after Brazil and Cuba had been pressured into banning slave imports.

The ultimate aim of the abolitionists was to end slavery in the Americas, but this was a far tougher task than ending the slave trade. Slave-owners could survive without importing fresh slaves, but they fought tooth and nail against freeing the workforce on which they believed their prosperity depended. Even many white people who opposed the slave trade saw the abolition of slavery itself as raising more complex issues, such as how to compensate slave-owners for the loss of their property and what to do with the freed slaves.

Free men consume more

British abolitionists frequently argued for the economic advantages of abolishing slavery. An anti-slavery pamphlet published in Liverpool in 1828 declared:

'The slaves in our West India islands, by being made free would not only raise more produce, but also consume much more of our manufactures.' (Quoted in Blackburn, *The Overthrow of Colonial Slavery*)

Slave uprisings

It was the actions of slaves themselves that shook the West Indian slave system to its roots. In the French colony of Saint Domingue (Haiti), a slave uprising in 1791, partly inspired by the ideals of the French Revolution, triggered a complex series of conflicts. The most prominent Haitian rebel, former slave Toussaint l'Ouverture, became a famous symbol of the freedom struggle. Toussaint was captured and died in France in 1803 as a prisoner of the Emperor Napoleon, but Haiti became independent the following year, the first black-ruled state in the New World.

Toussaint's example haunted plantation owners and colonial governments. There were further major slave revolts in the Caribbean, culminating in the Jamaican uprising of 1831-2. Led by Samuel 'Daddy' Sharpe, a slave inspired by Christian belief, it was put down only with the greatest difficulty and considerable bloodshed.

Top: A dramatic scene from the slave revolt against the French colonial authorities in St Domingue (modern-day Haiti).

Left: Toussaint l'Ouverture, a freed slave, became the leader of the black independence movement in St Domingue.

Abolition in British and French colonies

The Jamaican uprising and its brutal suppression gave further ammunition to abolitionists in Britain who were mounting a new mass campaign, this time calling for an end to slavery itself. Under intense popular pressure, the government brought in legislation to abolish slavery in the British colonies, with effect from 1 August 1834. However, slave-owners were paid a large sum in compensation and allowed to keep control of their former slaves as 'apprentices' for six years.

In France, the fate of abolition depended on the twists and turns of national politics. A French revolutionary government abolished slavery in the French colonies in 1794, but it was reimposed after Napoleon came to power in 1802, and maintained by the French kings who followed him. It was not until another revolution in Paris in 1848 that slaves in the French colonies were finally freed.

Dying for freedom

The Jamaican slave uprising of 1831-2, sometimes known as the Baptist War, ended with the defeat of the slaves and many executions. Surrounded by the rifles of British troops, one rebel leader, Patrick Ellis, refused to surrender and called on them to shoot:

'I am ready; give me your volley. Fire, for I will never again be a slave!'
(Quoted in Fryer, *Black People in the British Empire*)

'I know what slaves feel'

In 1831 British anti-slavery campaigners persuaded an escaped West Indian slave, Mary Prince, to publish her life story. In her immensely influential book, she eloquently denounced the often-repeated view that slaves were loyal and contented:

'How can slaves be happy when they have the halter round their neck and the whip upon their back and are disgraced and thought no more of than beasts? ... I have been a slave myself – I know what slaves feel ... The man that says slaves be quite happy in slavery – and that they don't want to be free – that man is either ignorant or a lying person. I never heard a slave say so.'
(Quoted in Blackburn, *The Overthrow of Colonial Slavery*)

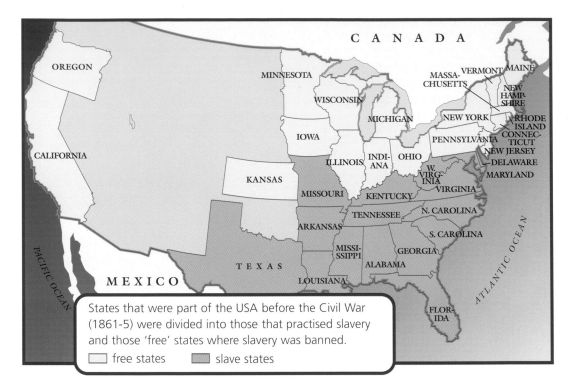

States that were part of the USA before the Civil War (1861-5) were divided into those that practised slavery and those 'free' states where slavery was banned.

☐ free states   ■ slave states

Slaves work the fields under close supervision.

Abolition in the USA

In the USA, the first half of the nineteenth century saw a deepening split between the Northern and Southern states. In the North, slavery was abolished everywhere by the early 1800s. In the South, however, slavery not only persisted but rapidly expanded. The number of slaves in the USA rose from about 1 million in 1800 to 4 million in 1860. The fast-growing British textile industry created an almost limitless demand for cotton, most of which was produced in the Southern USA by slave labour. Although some new slaves were still smuggled into the USA after the ban on slave imports in 1808, the need for growing numbers of slaves to pick the cotton was mostly met through natural reproduction – more slaves were born than died. For some slave-owners, a major source of profit came from their slaves having children, who could later be sold to work in the cotton fields. By 1860 cotton accounted

Encouraging child-bearing

Former slave Frederick Douglass became a distinguished figure in the American abolitionist movement. In his account of his life as a slave, published in 1845, he described how one slave-holder in Maryland cynically set out to increase his human property:

'Mr Covey ... was only able to buy one slave; and, shocking as is the fact, he bought her, as he said, for a breeder. This woman was named Caroline ... She was a large, able-bodied woman, about twenty years old ... After buying her, he hired a married man ... to live with him one year; and him he used to fasten up with her every night! The result was that, at the end of the year, the miserable woman gave birth to twins. At this result Mr Covey seemed to be highly pleased ... The children were regarded as being quite an addition to his wealth.' (Douglass, *Narrative of the Life of Frederick Douglass*)

for more than half of all the export trade of the USA. The Southern 'cottonocracy' saw slavery as essential to their business and to the economy.

As in the West Indies, the slave system in the USA was challenged by slave uprisings, the most notable led by Nat Turner in Virginia in 1831. There was also an influential abolitionist movement led by white liberals in the North. The American Anti-Slavery Society, founded in 1833 by William Lloyd Garrison, successfully kept the slavery issue in the forefront of public debate. But the most active opponents of slavery were freed or escaped slaves living in the North. They were the main organizers of the 'Underground Railroad' which served as an escape route for slaves from the South to the North. The formidable Harriet Tubman was one of the most active organizers of the 'Railroad', frequently crossing into the South to lead slaves to freedom. Perhaps a thousand a year escaped across the Ohio River.

Harriet Tubman (c. 1820-1913) escaped from slavery in Maryland in 1849. She helped other slaves escape from the South via the 'Underground Railroad'. In the Civil War she was a spy for the North.

As pressure for the abolition of slavery mounted, slave-owners in the Southern USA had a pressing interest in improving the image of slavery. There was increasing public disapproval of gross mistreatment of slaves. Southern slave-owners presented an image of themselves as benevolent patriarchs surrounded by devoted blacks for whose welfare they cared. They stressed their paternal role towards the slaves, who were now often envisaged more as irresponsible children than as dangerous savages. In a typical argument, Governor Hammond of South Carolina described plantation life as warm-hearted compared with the free-enterprise industrial society of the North. 'In this cold, calculating, ambitious world of ours,' he wrote, 'there are few ties more heartfelt, or of more benign influence, than those which mutually bind the master and the slave.'

By contrast, abolitionists sought to influence public opinion by publicizing the brutal side of life on the Southern plantations, most

Owned by her slaves

Visiting a plantation in South Carolina in 1856, Frederick Law Olmsted was told that the planter's wife had recently stayed up all night to look after a slave who was giving birth. Aware that slave ownership was under attack, the planter's wife said:

'It is the slaves who own me. Morning, noon and night, I'm obliged to look after them, to doctor them, and attend to them in every way.'
(Quoted in Genovese, *Roll, Jordan, Roll: The World the Slaves Made*)

Harriet Beecher Stowe (1811-96) and a poster for her best-selling novel, which vividly portrayed the brutal side of life on plantations in the American South.

135,000 SETS, 270,000 VOLUMES SOLD.

UNCLE TOM'S CABIN

OR SALE HERE.

...TION FOR THE MILLION, COMPLETE IN 1 Vol., PRICE 37 1-2 CENTS.
...IN GERMAN, IN 1 Vol., PRICE 50 CENTS.
...2 Vols., CLOTH, 6 PLATES, PRICE $1.50.
...TION IN 1 Vol., WITH 153 ENGRAVINGS,

influentially in Harriet Beecher Stowe's melodramatic best-selling novel *Uncle Tom's Cabin*, published in 1852.

As debate raged, the majority of people in the northern USA remained content for slavery to continue in the South, as long as they felt they could keep it out of the North. How acceptable slavery was to the majority of white Americans is shown by the fact that 11 of the 16 presidents of the USA elected up to 1860 were slave-owners.

The American Civil War

Conflict between the 'free' and 'slave' states focused on two issues. One concerned new territory being added to the USA as it expanded: should new states allow slavery or not? In 1854, Kansas and Nebraska, preparing to join the Union, were given the right to decide for themselves on the slavery issues. As a result, 'Bleeding Kansas' became literally a battleground between pro- and anti-slavers, with both sides prepared to kill for their cause. The other crucial issue was whether slaves could be held in free states. In 1857, in the 'Dred Scott case', the US Supreme Court ruled that a slave-holder who brought a slave into a free state still had full rights over his 'property'. This raised fears that the institution of slavery might spread to states that did not want it.

Northerners increasingly felt that a choice was being forced on the USA. Abraham Lincoln, the successful Republican candidate in the 1860 presidential election, spoke for many when he said: 'I believe this government cannot endure, permanently half slave and half free.' Lincoln's election precipitated the withdrawal of the Southern states from the Union and, as a result, civil war between the North and the South.

Good as they get

Although some slaves felt loyalty and attachment to their masters, most retained a deep scepticism even about the kindest of them. After emancipation, a former slave from the Southern USA commented on the woman who had once owned her:

'She was the best white woman that ever broke bread, but you know, honey, that wasn't much, 'cause they all hated the po' nigger.'
(Quoted in Genovese, *Roll, Jordan, Roll: The World the Slaves Made*)

Abraham Lincoln, sixteenth president of the USA (1861-5).

Letter from a free man

During the American Civil War many slaves escaped from their owners and fled to the North to offer their services to the Unionist forces. One escaped slave from Maryland wrote to his wife, who had stayed behind:

'My Dear Wife, It is with great joy I take this time to let you know where I am. I am now in safety in the 14th Regiment of Brooklyn. This day I can address you, thank god, as a free man. I had a little trouble in getting away. But as the Lord led the children of Israel to the land of Canaan, so he led us to a land where freedom will reign in spite of earth and hell.'
(Quoted in Fields et. al, ed, *Freedom: A Documentary History*)

The North did not fight the war as a crusade against slavery, but to uphold the unity of the USA. Many slaves, however, seized the opportunity to desert their Southern masters, and black regiments fought for the Unionist cause. The slaves themselves turned the war into a liberation struggle. In 1863, as a tactical measure in the war, Lincoln declared slaves free in the Southern states. This Emancipation Proclamation had no practical effect, as it only concerned areas over which Lincoln had no control. But by the end of the war sentiment in the

Deserted by his slaves

Many slave-owners in the American South had convinced themselves that they were loved and admired by their slaves. Their illusions were shattered when the civil war came and slaves leapt at the chance to fight for their freedom. Louis Marrigault, one of the largest plantation owners in the Deep South, wrote in 1862:

'This war has taught us the perfect impossibility of placing the least confidence in the negro. In too numerous instances those we esteemed the most have been the first to desert us.'
(Quoted in Genovese, *Roll, Jordan, Roll: The World the Slaves Made*)

North had turned overwhelmingly against allowing slavery to continue. After the Unionist victory in 1865 the 13th amendment to the US constitution formally abolished slavery in the USA.

Union before abolition

President Lincoln was more concerned with preserving the USA than with the abolition of slavery. In 1862, during the civil war, he wrote:

'If I could save the Union without freeing any slave I would do it; and if I could do it by freeing all the slaves I would do it; and if I could do it by freeing some and leaving the others alone, I would do that.'

Photographs like these, of an escaped slave turned 'Drummer Jackson', were circulated as propaganda to persuade slaves to fight for the North.

End of an era

The last major country practising slavery in the Americas was Brazil. Unable to hold out against the almost universal disapproval of world opinion, the Brazilians finally freed their slaves in 1888. The era of slavery in the Americas was at an end – but the problems it left behind were still unsolved more than a century later.

THE AFTERMATH OF SLAVERY

Like this young boy from a rural town in Mississippi, many African Americans were still living in poverty by the end of the twentieth century.

The abolition of slavery left the Americas with a large population of free citizens of African origin. There were some small efforts by abolitionists to arrange for the return of freed slaves to Africa – especially by the British to Sierra Leone from the 1780s, and by the Americans to Liberia from the 1820s. But these limited gestures did not alter the fact that the forced migration from Africa had added a major new element to the population of the New World, and that African Americans were there to stay.

It is conceivable that the abolition of slavery might have been followed by a determined effort to help former slaves build successful lives as free men and women, and to integrate them into economic and political life. But this is not what happened. Instead, whites took measures to exclude blacks from political rights and to ensure that they continued to serve the economic interests of their former masters. Enduring inequality based on colour became a fundamental fact of life in the Americas. Even in Brazil, where a formal colour bar did not exist, society was generally graded from the whitest skins in the highest social class to the blackest in the lowliest.

Poor but free

For many African Americans freedom from slavery brought no improvement in their conditions of life; for some there was even greater hardship. Former Alabama slave Stephen McCroy explained his own attitude to this with a story:

'Every time I think of slavery and if it done the race [African Americans] any good, I think of the story of the racoon and the dog who met. The racoon said to the dog: "Why is it you're so fat and I am so poor, and we is both animals?" The dog said: "I lay round Master's house and let him kick me and he gives me a piece of bread right on." Said the racoon to the dog: "Better then that I stay poor." '
(Quoted in Genovese, *Roll, Jordan, Roll: The World the Slaves Made*)

Unfit to be free

Infected with a racist contempt for blacks, many white people believed that slaves were unfit for freedom. In 1834, on the eve of the abolition of slavery in the British Empire, officials of the British Colonial Office were worried that freed slaves might become idle. An official memorandum said:

'A state of things in which the negro escaped the necessity for ... labour would be as bad for him as for his owner. He would be cut off from civilizing influences, would have no incentive to better his condition or to impose but the slightest degree of discipline on himself. Thus he might well become a more degraded being than his ancestors in Africa.'
(Quoted in Blackburn, *The Overthrow of Colonial Slavery*)

In the British West Indies the 'apprenticeship' system, intended to keep the former slaves working on their plantations for six years after abolition, soon broke down after protests and acts of resistance. Most former slaves wanted to buy land and establish themselves as free farmers, while the plantation owners did what they could to block their access to land and force them to work on the plantations for low pay. In the end, the plantation owners partly replaced the slaves by importing indentured labourers, in effect semi-slaves, from India. About 300,000 were shipped to the British West Indies in the second half of the nineteenth century.

Meanwhile many former slaves achieved their ambition of owning a plot of land, with difficulty extracting a living from the soil, but at least enjoying their independence. More than a century passed before black West Indians started to wrest political power from their colonial masters, gaining first a measure of self-government and then, from the 1960s, full independence for their island nations.

Gradually, in the latter part of the twentieth century, African Americans came to hold positions in government – like Condoleeza Rice, who became US National Security Advisor in 2000.

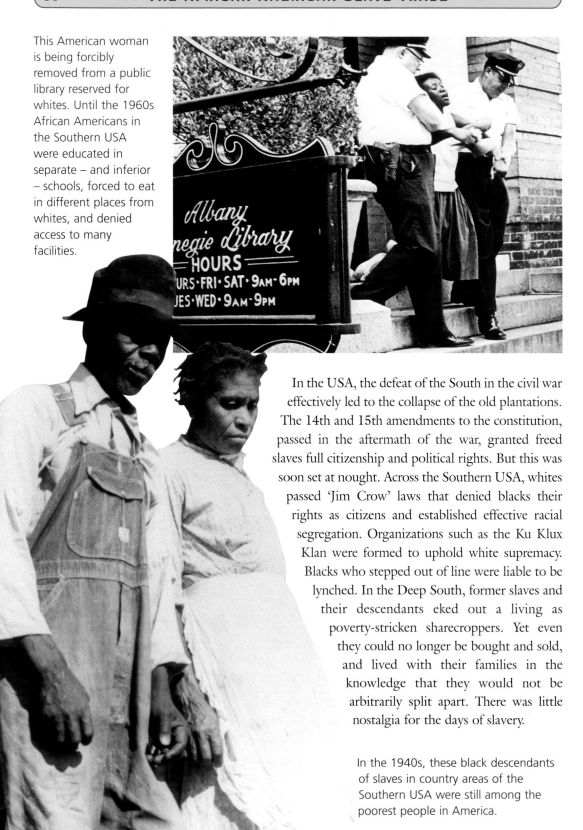

This American woman is being forcibly removed from a public library reserved for whites. Until the 1960s African Americans in the Southern USA were educated in separate – and inferior – schools, forced to eat in different places from whites, and denied access to many facilities.

In the USA, the defeat of the South in the civil war effectively led to the collapse of the old plantations. The 14th and 15th amendments to the constitution, passed in the aftermath of the war, granted freed slaves full citizenship and political rights. But this was soon set at nought. Across the Southern USA, whites passed 'Jim Crow' laws that denied blacks their rights as citizens and established effective racial segregation. Organizations such as the Ku Klux Klan were formed to uphold white supremacy. Blacks who stepped out of line were liable to be lynched. In the Deep South, former slaves and their descendants eked out a living as poverty-stricken sharecroppers. Yet even they could no longer be bought and sold, and lived with their families in the knowledge that they would not be arbitrarily split apart. There was little nostalgia for the days of slavery.

In the 1940s, these black descendants of slaves in country areas of the Southern USA were still among the poorest people in America.

The effect on Africa

In Africa, the ending of the Atlantic slave trade forced changes on the slave-trading states along the west coast. Some west African rulers and traders made a quite successful adjustment, replacing the trade in slaves with the export of products such as palm oil and rubber. But the gap between the technology and power of European and African countries was widening dramatically. Europeans were increasingly inclined to see Africa as an open field for exploration, missionary work and economic exploitation.

From the 1830s, British abolitionists launched a crusade to end slavery in Africa and stop the trade in African slaves to the Muslim Middle East, which still flourished, especially along Africa's east coast. The anti-slavery cause became a major justification for the European powers to intervene in African affairs and humiliate African rulers. By the 1890s, the European states had taken control of almost the entire continent, carving it up between them without reference to the people who lived there. The European imperialists' conviction that they could 'civilize' Africa had a sourly hypocritical feel to those who had been victims of the Atlantic slave trade.

Black consciousness

The growth of the civil rights movement and the raising of 'black consciousness' in the USA from the late 1950s brought the slavery question back into the limelight of public debate. Facts of history at the time familiar to few Americans became widely known – for example, that the family names used by many African Americans were in fact the names of the slave masters who had owned their slave ancestors; or the fact, highlighted at the start of this book, that many of the country's founding fathers had been slave-owners. In the 1970s the televising of black American Alex Haley's best-seller *Roots*, about his search for his family's origins in Africa, had a major impact on African Americans – there was soon a thriving tourist trade taking black Americans to West Africa.

American civil rights campaigner Alex Haley embarked on a search for his family origins which led him to a village in Gambia, West Africa. Here, one of his African relatives holds his picture.

In January 2001, US President Bill Clinton presented a medal of honour to the grandson of Corporal Andrew Jackson Smith, a former slave. The medal was in recognition of Corporal Smith's role in a battle in the Civil War.

An unequal legacy

Slavery became a key factor in attempts by black radicals to explain the fact of enduring racial inequality in the USA. The impact of slavery was seen as so dreadful and dehumanizing that it left even future generations scarred. Radicals began to refer to the slave trade as the African Holocaust, likening it to the Nazis' attempted extermination of the Jews in Europe during the Second World War. Some historians have responded by pointing out that much that shocks us about the slave trade is less sensational seen in the context of its time. For example, the death rate of slaves crossing the Atlantic was barely higher than that of the ships' crews, since until the 1800s all sea voyages were hazardous and plagued by disease. Nor, they argue, was the treatment of slaves on plantations consistently any worse than that of free workers in factories at the same period. Nonetheless, at the World Conference on Racism in 2001, the USA and European countries came under pressure to apologise for the suffering and exploitation of slavery and to pay financial compensation to Africans and African Americans. They did neither.

Redress for wrong

In 1997 the *People's Tribune*, the magazine of the radical League of Revolutionaries for a New America, argued that the US government should apologise for slavery and pay reparations to black Americans:

'We know that slavery was morally wrong. So the question boils down to this: Does the government regret upholding such terrible exploitation and oppression while preaching democracy to the rest of the world? ... Does the government regret its role of legalizing the attempt to torture a people and beat them down to the level of a draft animal?'
(*People's Tribune*, August 1997)

Beneficiaries of servitude

Booker T. Washington, a prominent black spokesman of the early twentieth century, called on his fellow African Americans to turn their backs on slavery and look to the future:

'We went into slavery pagans; we came out Christians. We went into slavery pieces of property; we came out American citizens ... Notwithstanding the cruelty and moral wrong of slavery, we are in a stronger and more hopeful condition ... than is true of an equal number of black people in any other portion of the globe.'
(Quoted in D'Souza, *The End of Racism*)

Present-day parallels

Pockets of slavery and many kinds of tied labour have continued to exist up to the present day in places across the world. But perhaps the closest contemporary equivalent to the Atlantic slave trade is the movement of illegal immigrants, driven by poverty to undertake hazardous journeys to distant countries short of labour. Although they were not strictly forced to migrate, the terrible fate of Chinese illegal immigrants suffocated to death in the back of a lorry crossing the English Channel in June 2000 does recall some of the horrors of the 'Middle Passage'. The Atlantic slave trade stands as a monumental example of inhumanity and the destructive power of greed. But it may be that, to some future generation, the poverty and inequality of our world will seem as self-evidently wrong as American slavery and the slave trade seem to us today.

A monument to remember the abolition of slavery in Puerto Rico in 1873, is also a reminder of what was suffered by so many.

DATE LIST

1441   Portuguese sailors bring captives back to Portugal from the west coast of Africa.

1481   Portugal establishes the first European fort on the West African coast at Elmina.

1502   The first African slaves are brought to the New World by the Portuguese.

1562   The first recorded English slave voyage is captained by John Hawkyns.

1600   The Portuguese colony of Brazil is the major importer of African slaves as sugar production expands.

1650-1720   The rise of sugar plantations in the British and French colonies in the West Indies gives a massive boost to the slave trade.

1660   Maryland is the first colony in North America to legally recognize slavery-for-life as the lot of African Americans.

1690   The Asante establish an empire in West Africa that will grow rich on the slave trade.

1772   Judgement in the Somerset case effectively means that a slave is free on landing in Britain.

1780   Pennsylvania votes to abolish slavery, though not with immediate effect.

1787   The anti-slavery society in Britain begins a mass campaign for the abolition of the slave trade.

1791   A slave uprising takes over the French colony of Saint Domingue (Haiti).

1794   French revolutionaries in Paris declare the abolition of slavery in France's colonies.

1802   French ruler Napoleon Bonaparte reintroduces slavery in the French colonies, but fails to restore French rule in Haiti.

1804   Denmark is the first European country to ban the slave trade.

1807   Britain declares an end to the slave trade.

1808   The import of slaves into the USA is banned.

1833   Slavery is abolished in the British Empire.

1848   After a revolution in Paris, slavery is abolished in the French Empire.

1854	The Kansas-Nebraska Act allows new states joining the USA to decide whether to be 'slave' or 'free'.
1857	A decision in the Dred Scott case says that a slave brought into a 'free' state of the USA remains a slave.
1861-5	The American Civil War is fought, in which slavery is a major issue.
1862	President Abraham Lincoln declares the emancipation of slaves in the Confederate states from 1 January 1863.
1866	The Thirteenth Amendment to the US Constitution outlaws slavery in the USA.
1867	The last recorded slave ship to cross the Atlantic lands its cargo in Cuba.
1888	Slavery is abolished in Brazil, two years after its abolition in Cuba.

RESOURCES

SOURCES

Sources of information for this book were:

Robin Blackburn, *The Making of New World Slavery*, Verso, 1997

Robin Blackburn, *The Overthrow of Colonial Slavery*, Verso, 1988

J. Winston Coleman Jr, *Slavery Times in Kentucky*, University of North Carolina Press, 1940

Michael Craton, *Sinews of Empire*, Maurice Temple Smith, 1974

Michael Craton, *Testing the Chains*, Cornell University Press, 1982

Frederick Douglass, *Narrative of the Life of Frederick Douglass, An American Slave*, Doubleday, 1989

Dinesh D'Souza, *The End of Racism*, The Free Press, 1995

Olaudah Equiano et al., *Slave Narratives*, Library of America, 2000

B. J. Fields et al. (eds), *Freedom, A Documentary History of Emancipation 1861-1867*, Cambridge University Press, 1985

Peter Fryer, *Black People in the British Empire*, Pluto Press, 1988

Eugene D. Genovese, *Roll, Jordan, Roll: The World the Slaves Made*, Andre Deutsch, 1974

Herbert S. Klein, *The Atlantic Slave Trade*, Cambridge University Press, 1999

Roland Oliver, *The African Experience*, Weidenfeld & Nicolson, 1991

James Pope-Hennessy, *Sins of the Fathers: The Atlantic Slave Trade 1441-1807*, Weidenfeld & Nicolson, 1967

Oliver Ransford, *The Slave Trade*, John Murray, 1971

Arthur L. Stinchcombe, *Sugar Island Slavery in the Age of Enlightenment*, Princeton University Press, 1995

Hugh Thomas, *The Slave Trade*, Picador, 1997

FURTHER INFORMATION

For those who feel that they can take on a popularly written but lengthy history book, Hugh Thomas's *The Slave Trade* can be recommended.

Of accounts written by slaves themselves, Frederick Douglass's *Narrative of the Life of Frederick Douglass* is available from good bookshops and interesting to read.

Alex Hayley's *Roots* is a popular book that especially fascinated many African Americans when it came out in the 1970s.

Among novels, few young people are likely to find Harriet Beecher Stowe's *Uncle Tom's Cabin* readable, but Mark Twain's *Huckleberry Finn* is still exciting, a classic adventure story set in the American South with slavery one of its central themes.

Steven Spielberg's movie *Amistad* is a worthy treatment of the issue of freedom and slavery.

Internet surfers will come upon plenty of information and debate, especially on the history of slavery in the USA. Two excellent websites are:
www.pbs.org   (Africans in America program)
www.spartacus.schoolnet.co.uk   (Slavery)

GLOSSARY

abolitionist   person in favour of banning slavery and the slave trade.

capital   money invested in a business in the hope of making a profit.

civil rights movement   a movement in the USA in the 1950s and 1960s demanding an end to discrimination against African Americans.

colony   a country ruled by another country as part of an empire.

colour bar   denying people rights because of the colour of their skin.

emancipation   the freeing of slaves.

evangelists   enthusiastic religious preachers, especially those active in the Anglican church in the late eighteenth century and early nineteenth century.

factor   a European or North American who was stationed in an African town or coastal fort, often acting as a go-between in the slave trade.

flux   eighteenth-century word for dysentery, a potentially fatal disease of the intestines.

gibbet   a wooden structure on which people were hanged to death or on which their dead bodies were exposed to public view.

human rights   freedoms that all humans should have the right to enjoy.

indigo   a plant producing a blue dye used to colour textiles for clothing.

Ku Klux Klan   a secret organization set up by whites in the Southern United States after the ending of slavery to uphold white domination.

maroons   escaped slaves living in remote parts of West Indian islands.

Methodist   a member of a Christian religious movement initially inspired by John Wesley (1703-91).

Middle Passage   term used for the voyage by slaving ships across the Atlantic.

mulatto   a person with one black and one white parent.

Negroes   word generally used to mean 'black people' until the end of the 1960s, when it came to be regarded as unacceptable.

New World   term used for the Americas, as opposed to the 'Old World' of Europe, Asia and Africa.

plantation   a large estate where crops such as sugar, coffee or tobacco were produced; the owner of a plantation was sometimes called a 'planter'.

Quakers   a Christian sect, founded by George Fox in 1650, which played a leading part in early moves to abolish slavery.

quarantine   system for keeping people arriving from abroad isolated for a while, so that they cannot bring infectious diseases into the country.

sub-Saharan Africa   all of Africa south of the Sahara desert, sometimes called 'black Africa'.

Unionist   in the American Civil War, a supporter of the Union against the attempt by the Southern Confederate states to quit the USA.

voodoo   a form of religion and magic practised in some Caribbean islands, combining elements of Catholicism and traditional African beliefs. The Brazilian version is called candomble.

INDEX